ELVIS
in Quotes

ELVIS
in Quotes

Sid Shaw

ELVISLY YOURS LTD.
BOX 315 LONDON NW10

Published by
Elvisly Yours Ltd
P.O. Box 315, London NW10, England.

copyright © Sid Shaw

ISBN 1-869941-02-0 (Hardback)

British Library Cataloguing in Publication Data

Shaw, Sid
    Elvis in Quotes
    1.   Presley, Elvis — Portraits, etc.
    2.   Singers — United States — Portraits
    I.   Title
    784,5'0092'4   Ml420.P96

Designed by: Sarah Goddard for
                E.T. Budge & Associates

Typesetter: JC Press, London NW5

Printed by: Philip Print Ltd
            London NW10 6NB

Bound by: R.J. Acford
          Chichester
          England

Reproduction: Bowman Litho Ltd, London
              Compliment Colour Services, London

Introduction

Elvis Presley:

What was he *really* like?

There have been hundreds of books written on Elvis Presley and yet we are no nearer knowing him or understanding why the world fell in love with him and referred to him by his first name:

ELVIS

There have been books written by "friends" and some of these within a few weeks of his death. All told the true story and these "friends" were the closest and Elvis confided everything to them. A friend would explain just what Elvis was like but in reality most of these books were ego trips and a way to make a "quick buck". The most trusted, the most loyal, the most dedicated friends have yet to write books and maybe they never will. They probably wouldn't want the harassment from the media with the launch of their book and to have to answer over and over again all the questions they have heard so many, many times. Perhaps we will get somewhere near understanding Elvis Presley when one of these true friends write their book as a labour of love and donate all their royalties to charity, a kind of Elvis Aid!

There have been books written by members of the family. Elvis didn't have any brothers or sisters (just a twin brother who died at birth). But he did have many cousins, uncles and aunts and many were on the payroll. Their books still do not explain the phenomenon of Elvis Presley. For the most part they are just sweet, easy reading and full of anecdotes. A book written by Elvis's stepbrother David Stanley is more hard-hitting, more blunt and more readable but it dwells more on David Stanley and less on Elvis Presley. David's *"Life with Elvis"* helps but is still not the answer. The closest family member, the most trusted confidant and the closest friend was Billy Smith and he

does not intend to write a book. Elvis Presley was his life, from the poverty stricken days in Tupelo where they were born, to making a living in Memphis, to those great early days in the 50s, to the films, the concerts and years on the road and until that fateful day on August 16th 1977. For the last two years of Elvis's life Billy was with him for 18 hours a day. His book would be the ultimate book on Elvis Presley but Billy just wants a peaceful life in a small sleepy town in Mississippi.

Then there have been the professionals who have tried to chronicle Elvis's life and death. To get to the real Elvis they would have had to question the family and friends. The close circle of Elvis's friends and family would not talk at length with someone researching a book on Elvis. It was either personal or they had their own book already in mind. So the professionals would just have a patchwork effect of Elvis's life and still we wouldn't understand the man. Yet, there have been some good attempts by professionals at analysing the life of Elvis

Presley and some *bad* attempts, notably by Albert Goldman. Much of the character assassination of Elvis Presley has stemmed from Goldman's book. It was serialised in newspapers and magazines all over the world. The world's press love scandal and what better than a vicious personal attack on the world's greatest star after he is dead and cannot fight back. It is very strange, but, Albert Goldman wrote an article in 1969 in *Life* Magazine in which he put Elvis Presley on a pedestal like a god. His article was full of praise and love and yet years later he wrote his nasty, infamous book . . .

I received a phone call from an Elvis fan at midnight one night in England. I begged the caller to wait until the morning but he insisted I had to hear a story immediately. The caller then proceeded to read from an article written about one of Elvis's concerts. After some paragraphs the fan asked me who I thought it was. I was rather tired but carried on listening to this very flowery, verbose account written by it seemed an Elvis groupie. I

said I thought it was some woman madly in love with Elvis. He read on and repeated the question. Again I said a woman in love with Elvis Presley. He finished the article and yet again asked the question and I gave the same answer. He hesitated, took a breath and then told me the article was written by Albert Goldman. I woke up! Goldman's book had already been serialised in the papers in Britain and the damage had been done but the next morning I got to work and put out a Press Release about the article in the papers and ended it by stating "hell hath no fury like a woman scorned" and this quote was picked up in the *London Evening Standard* and I was then taken to task by Britain's *Gay News*.

Was Goldman's book a real in depth analysis of the legend of Elvis Presley or was Goldman in love with Elvis and scorned? Perhaps Elvis wouldn't give him an interview or one of the guards was rough with Albert. We will never know. Whereas John Lennon was assassinated by a fan with a gun, Goldman chose the pen. It was based on

supposedly hundreds of interviews with the family and associates and two of those named interviewees George Klein and Jerry Schilling sued Albert Goldman for $40 million. They were never interviewed by Goldman and disgusted that their names were listed as contributors to such a wicked attack on their friend. The lawsuit was dropped because it was felt that dragging the case through the courts would just give even more publicity to Goldman and keep the nasty book in the headlines and just make more money for Goldman. Although his book made Goldman a rich man we still do not know the real Elvis Presley. Goldman's book just distorted the story of Elvis with lies and half truths and it didn't even recognise Elvis's musical talent. Read that article in *Life* Magazine reproduced in No. 1 of *Elvisly Yours* Magazine.

Many fans and fan clubs have written books on Elvis. For the most part they are labours of love with very little money behind them and no marketing and promotion. In many cases only one or two thousand books were ever printed. One series of fans books stand head and shoulders above many of the rest and these are by Sean Shaver. A fan who followed Elvis around his concerts and took some superb photographs. Sean's books leave a lot to be desired in the way of text but the books are beautifully produced and they captured a unique part of Elvis's life on film, when Elvis was doing what he loved most — performing and knocking them dead. The previous book by Elvisly Yours called *Elvis, A King Forever* or in some countries just *Elvis* was written by Rob Gibson and assisted by Sid Shaw. It tried to tell the simple story of Elvis's life in words and pictures for the fan, the music buff, the student (an interesting diary of events complements the text) or just the Elvis voyeur. It has been highly praised by not only the fans but by many of Elvis's close family and friends. But still it does not really explain Elvis Presley and why there will never be another like him.

Surely the book by his ex-wife, Priscilla, would be the ultimate book on Elvis and a real insight would be grasped of what Elvis was like, what made him tick, how he related to his daughter Lisa. For the first fifty pages or so it was fascinating reading, but then it jumped in leaps and bounds through Elvis's life. It seemed as if the book was just rushed into print to justify the enormous advances made to Priscilla. I and most of the Elvis World hoped the book would explain the man, his hopes, his fears, his loves, his hates but all it did was to raise more questions. Elvis was very close to his wider family and especially his cousin Billy and Jo Smith (Jo was like a sister to Priscilla) and yet she practically ignored them in her book and since Elvis died. What happened to Elvis in the 70's and the concert years? Although they were divorced there was communication, yet the book gives very little detail. What will happen to Graceland? Why, oh why did Priscilla not

discuss the intimate relationship Elvis had with Lisa Marie? Generally, fans all over the world were upset by her book. Some praised it but the general feeling was that in life she would have never made public intimate sexual details of her life with Elvis so why do it when Elvis is dead. So still we do not know the real Elvis Presley.

Alas we may have to wait until the historians really get to study and understand the Legend of Elvis Presley. There have been some academic books on Elvis and the best by far is by Patsy Guy Hammontree called *Elvis: A Bio-Bibliography*. It is the most objective book ever written on Elvis being an academic treatise for University students. As an academic book it had a limited print run and was not generally available. Eventually there will be the ultimate book on Elvis, or rather there will be an encyclopedia of books. There are probably historians and sociologists now working on such a project and when completed we may finally understand the Elvis Presley phenomenon. How is it that one man captured the hearts of millions of people all over the world ... from Singapore to Iceland from Australia to Brazil everyone knows the name Elvis and he has sold over one billion records. No one will ever get near him as a recording star and no one will ever change the face of society so dramatically as Elvis Presley. Yet the impact he had on the 20th Century and with all the books and films and documentaries we still do not know what he was really like and so we come to *Elvis In Quotes*.

So much had been written but so little has been said about Elvis Presley. Over the years I have collected an enormous range of photos of Elvis and published them in our highly praised Elvisly Yours Magazine. I always wanted to produce the best of Elvisly Yours as a compilation of our best photographs. I have been to Memphis twenty four times from England and on a recent visit was even presented with the Keys to the City of Memphis. Each visit I have managed to add to my collection of photographs. Elvis Presley was probably the world's most photographed man. Millions of fans took millions of photographs. Then there were photographers, photo agencies, family and friends and still there are millions of photographs yet to be published. I always felt that the vast majority of books on Elvis have had a very poor selection of photographs and our first book *Elvis, A King Forever* helped to redress the balance with a great photo portfolio. *Elvis In Quotes* would continue that tradition but we needed a good text to accompany the best of our photographs. I always felt you can learn a lot about a person from what other people said about them and what they said themselves. I had met most of Elvis's close family and friends over the years. We had invited to England members of the Memphis Mafia and some members of

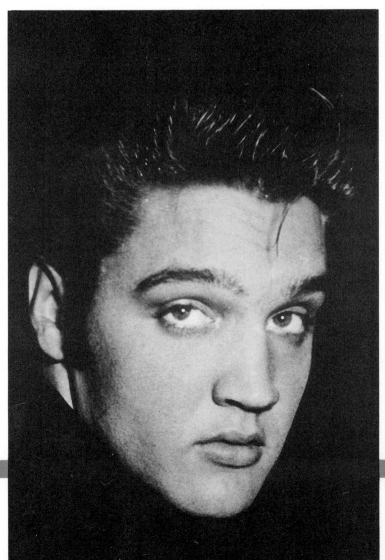

Elvis's family. But I wanted to know what people other than associates and relatives thought about him and had planned to begin a major research project. I had planned to write to famous people for a quote on Elvis and piece together their quotes and my photographs. As fate had it and a lot of luck one day Jackie Lynton walked into my office with an armful of quotes. He totally independently had been collecting quotes on Elvis as a hobby and thought it would be nice to get them published. I am indebted to Jackie Lynton for the research on the quotes which have been taken from newspapers, magazines, radio and TV interviews over many years. It was a labour of love from one fan who is in the music business and in-between gigs working with top recording artists in Britain kept adding to his unique collection of Elvis quotes.

At the end of reading this book and admiring the very many rare photographs of Elvis I hope it will help you to understand the true meaning of the man and why Elvis Aaron Presley made more people happy than anyone else in history. *Elvis In Quotes* is just a taster because there are hundreds more quotes and hundreds more photographs. The problem was who to include and who to leave out and I apologise if anyone famous has been excluded. Maybe they will make it in the next volume. The simplest and most recent quote was from Elvis's close friend George Klein, who has done more than anyone to keep the memory of Elvis alive: "Elvis Now and Forever — Long Live the King". When we are all long gone they will still be singing his songs and watching his movies and videos and reading about the man they called the "King of Rock 'N' Roll".

Elvisly Yours,

Sid Shaw

I've heard it said that the lurchin, urchin, Elvis the Pelvis, hasn't any kind of singing voice, and I was anxious to hear if there was anything in the rumor. Frankly after 16 of his rock and roll ballads, delivered with a ferocious intensity and manoeuvres known in the burlesque business as "all-out grinds and bumps", I still have no way of knowing. I just didn't hear one note or one word he sang. 15,000 screaming youngsters for 1½ hours just wouldn't let me. He lays it on like a bulldozer in mating season.

HUGH THOMSON/Music Reviewer/Toronto Daily Star/1957

23

I don't want him on my show, I don't care what anyone says about him - how great a talent he is - he just won't be in my show and that's that.

ED SULLIVAN

Don't let anyone tell you that I made the boy what he is today. The kids are the ones who made Elvis, without them, he'd still be driving a truck.
COLONEL TOM-PARKER 1956

He sat on his butt in the snow like the rest of us and ate the same crummy food we did, he was a real Joe.
ARMY BUDDY

The news of his death absolutely stunned me, I stopped drinking. It's too easy to drink - so many things are available - in the world of rock music.
ELTON JOHN

I was priviledged to be a friend of Elvis Presley I can think of no greater hero in our city, no greater name, no greater contributor to the welfare of more people.
BILL MORRIS/Shelby County Mayor

I was always a little girl to him.
PRISCILLA

*E*lvis Presleys death deprives our country of a part of itself, his music and his personality fusing the styles of white country and black rythmn and blues, permanently changed the face of American popular culture. His following was immense and he was a symbol to the people the world over of the vitality, rebelliousness and good humor of this country. Elvis may be gone but his legend will be with us for a long time to come.

President JIMMY CARTER/1977

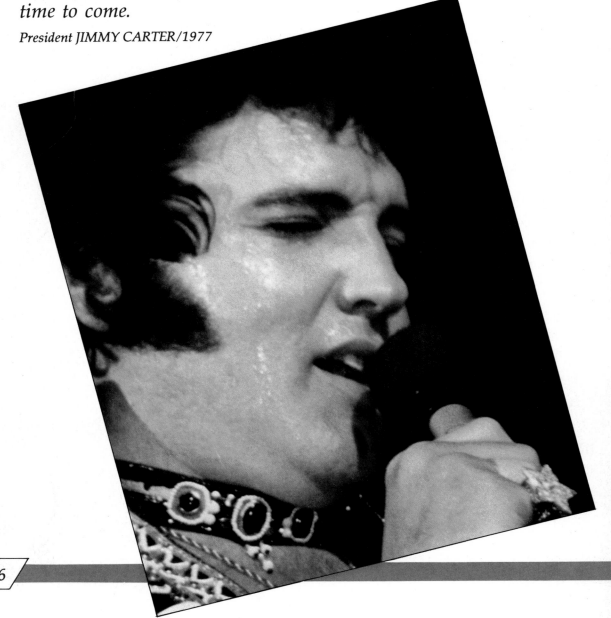

*W*hen he met President Nixon the President looked at Elvis's outfit, (Elvis was dressed in a solid black outfit with a huge black cape. He carried a black walking stick and wore an enormous gold belt) and said, Boy you sure do dress kind of wild, Elvis said Mr President you've got you show to run and I've got mine.

MARTY LACKER

I've known Elvis Presley almost ever since he came out. They brought him into Norfolk (Virginia). I remember they paid him $53 and he came in with Hank Snow — that was the first time I ever met him, he's a real fine guy.

GENE VINCENT/Rock 'n' Roll singer

One afternoon, he was eating breakfast, and on comes Robert Goulet on the big television set, very slowly Elvis finishes what he has in his mouth, puts down his knife and fork, picks up a .22 and – boom – blasts old Robert clean off the screen.

SONNY WEST/Bodyguard

*E*lvis was one of Hollywood's biggest and best practical jokers.

HOWARD SMITH/Make-Up Man/Hollywood

I had a T.V. show in Odessa, Texas, and we played mainly country music. But after Presley came through town for a show in late 1954 I began to notice the rythmn music, I hope that nobody will ever forget how he influenced us all – he isn't just a historical phenomenon, but rather something very lasting.

ROY ORBISON

I've lost a very dear friend and the world has lost a great entertainer.
ANN MARGRET/1977

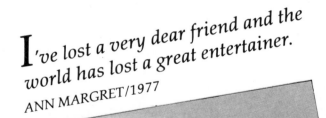

He is very polite, but not so cool that it prevents you from making conversation.
BRIAN WILSON/Beach Boys

When Elvis first came in I wondered if he wanted a handout. We get a lot of drifters here along Union Ave. He just said he wanted to sing.
MARION KEISKER/
Office Manager Sun Recording Co.

I know that the Lord can give, and the Lord can take away, I might be herding sheep next year.
ELVIS/1956

Elvis was a phenomenon of enormous proportion. It was Elvis who ended the languishing big band era and replaced it with something so popular that we are still in it's grips. The Beatles claimed to owe everything to Elvis. Around the world; he is still the archetypal image for rock'n'roll and it's singers. Few performers have won the devotion of so many or had such wide and lasting influence.

THE ROANOKE TIMES AND WORLD NEWS/1977

*H*e's cheerful enough, but Elvis just doesn't seem to have any genuine fun anymore, what I'm convinced he needs is another marriage then maybe Elvis - and all the rest of us - could go back to having a good time again.

PRESLEY AIDE/1974

*A*lthough I predict that 1976 is going to be a new beginning for Elvis Presley in the long run he is doomed, his inside outside battle will rage more and more without him being able to gain control, his greatest hope for salvation rests in his actions to get the proper psychological help now.

COUNT JOHN MANOLESCO/
Astrologer/1976

*T*here are a lot of people throughout the country who have their doubts as to whether Elvis Presley really died in August, 1977.

AL JEFFRIES/Researcher Fort Lauderdale

I watched the audience as he walked out on stage, and so many had their faces in their hands, they'd sit there and cry, it was almost biblical, as if the clouds had parted and down a shaft of light came the angels.

BILL JOST/Assistant Manager International Hotel

*H*e was a precious gift from God.

VERNON PRESLEY/Elvis' Dad

I saw him do things for kids that he'd die if he knew I was telling you about. He sent $5,000 to a hospital for retarded children in Ft. Worth, Texas. He had read in the newspaper during the four days we were in that city that a hospital needed money to buy games and toys for those kids, he spends, over $30,000 every Xmas to have bundles of gifts delivered to about five orphanages in different parts of the country. He's been doing that for the last 10 years.

NEVADA HOTEL OWNER/1974

*H*e was a haunted man almost necessarily, I felt sorry for him, because when I visited him I thought I was visiting an exile of some kingdom.

PAT BOONE/1977

*H*e liked hamburger steaks, string beans, creamed potato and roast beef.

MARY JENKINS/Elvis's Cook

*E*lvis represented a particular time in life and now it's gone forever.

THOMAS CAMPBELL/Vanderbilt Assistant Pro. of Psychology.

*I*f I had to find one place to live, just one, and it couldn't be Graceland, then it would have to be Hawaii.

ELVIS

*W*ithout Elvis, none of us could have made it.

BUDDY HOLLY

*T*he loss of Priscilla was the biggest blow to Elvis' ego. To go off with another man - that was the mortal blow.

ED PARKER/Karate Teacher

The mystery deepens as to what does Elvis Presley do when he isn't actually in front of a camera. Next to Howard Hughes, Elvis is rapidly becoming our leading recluse. He goes from set to home, from home to set as pleasant as he is to co-workers he never lunches in the studio commissaries or at any of the Los Angeles restaurants.

LOUELLA PARSONS/*Hollywood Gossip Writer*

45

Gorgeous — or some equally effusive effeminate word is the only way to describe Elvis Presley's latest epiphany at Las Vegas, not since Marlene Dietrich stunned the ringsider's with the sight of those legs encased from hip to ankle in a transparent gown, has any performer so electrified this jaded town with a personal appearance.

ALBERT GOLDMAN/1969

There's no denying the sheer physical power of this boy, at 21 he gives the impression he has lived for forty years.

ELIZABETH SCOTT/Co Star Loving You

I think he wants to come to England, but the Colonel just wants to wait a while longer.

FREDDIE BIENSTOCK/Head of Carlin Music

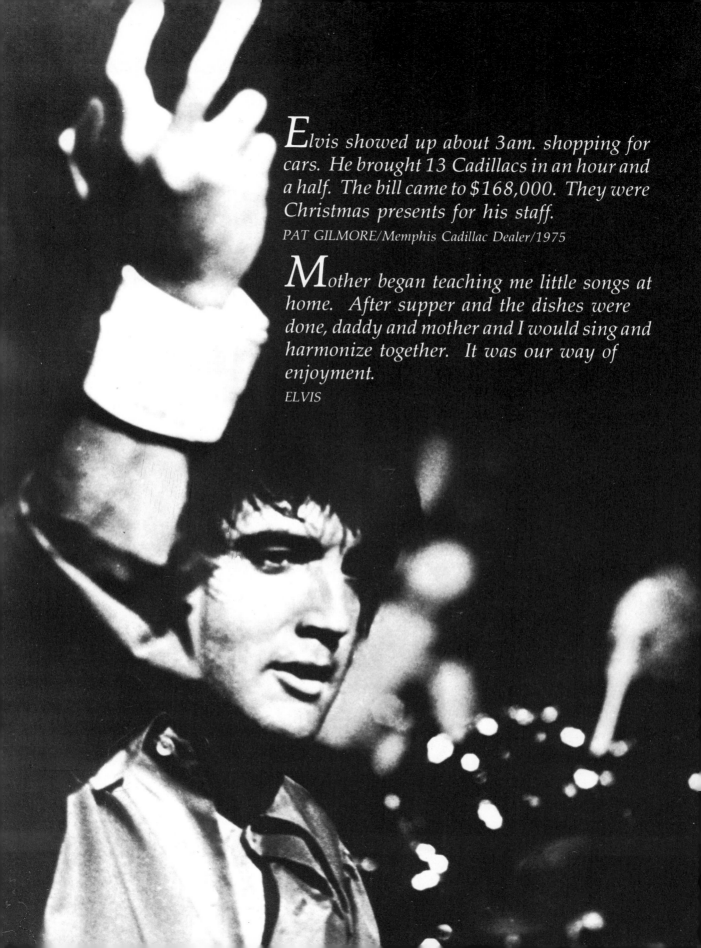

Elvis showed up about 3am. shopping for cars. He brought 13 Cadillacs in an hour and a half. The bill came to $168,000. They were Christmas presents for his staff.
PAT GILMORE/Memphis Cadillac Dealer/1975

Mother began teaching me little songs at home. After supper and the dishes were done, daddy and mother and I would sing and harmonize together. It was our way of enjoyment.
ELVIS

*O*nce Elvis tried unsuccessfully to convince a group of people outside a Memphis disco that he really was Elvis Presley. Because no one expected Elvis Presley to be out in public.

CHARLIE HODGE/Elvis aide and singer

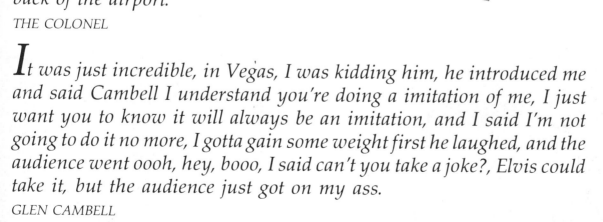

I was once waiting to board a plane with Elvis in Denver. Elvis disappeared, I couldn't find him anywhere, after a search, and in the nick of time, I found him pitching pennies with a taxi driver in the back of the airport.

THE COLONEL

*I*t was just incredible, in Vegas, I was kidding him, he introduced me and said Cambell I understand you're doing a imitation of me, I just want you to know it will always be an imitation, and I said I'm not going to do it no more, I gotta gain some weight first he laughed, and the audience went oooh, hey, booo, I said can't you take a joke?, Elvis could take it, but the audience just got on my ass.

GLEN CAMBELL

He is the most co-operative actor I ever met, he always stopped for fans, to give autographs, even though I knew he was worrying about the next scene.

NORMAN TAUROG/Director G.I. Blues

There is one thing Elvis can do better than any other actor I've worked with - that is put anyone famous or unknown, completely at their ease.

ROBERT A. RELYEA/Assistant Director
Jailhouse Rock

I was in his dressing room, and it was the most beautifully emotional thing I have ever seen between two men. The Colonel came down after showtime into the room. He just said, Where is he? The Colonel had tears in his eyes. His face was twisted in emotion I had never seen him like that before. I was with Joe Esposito and we pointed inside, Elvis came out. The Colonel took one step forward and so did Elvis. There were no words, they just put their arms around each other in a big hug. The Colonel had his back to me and I knew it was a private thing where we shouldn't hang around. We excused ourselves. But the Colonel's body was shaking with emotion. It was a beautiful moment.

CHARLIE HODGE/Las Vegas Hilton/July 31st 1969

Elvis has to be one of the greatest, if not the greatest, entertainers ever. When you book Elvis, you always know automatically that you have a sellout. I've never known of a show he's done anywhere that wasn't sold out.

BUBBA BAND/Memphis Mid South Coliseum Manager

He was different. He had a different style, a different talk, different walk, he definitely was a true one-of-a-kind.

CHET ATKINS

I'm still bewildered. Last night's contortionist exhibition at the auditorium was the closest to the jungle I'll ever get.

HELEN PARMELER/
Ottawa Journal/
1957

*F*urther proof that his popularity was stronger than ever was testified to by the fact that his 12 day tour of the northeast and south, to have begun the day after he died, was completely sold out.

JOHN RAFFA/Writer/A Salute to the King 1977

*O*n one occasion, a leather-clad member of a motorcycle gang drove his Harley to the gate, dismounted, tied a single black ribbon to one of the musical notes and then roared away.

JOHN FILIATREAU/Rock Writer 16th August 1977

*E*lvis was a man of many parts, many faces. While he sang spirituals in his act, offstage he was haunted by the fear of death and the afterlife.

JOE ESPOSITO

*B*efore Elvis there was nothing.

JOHN LENNON

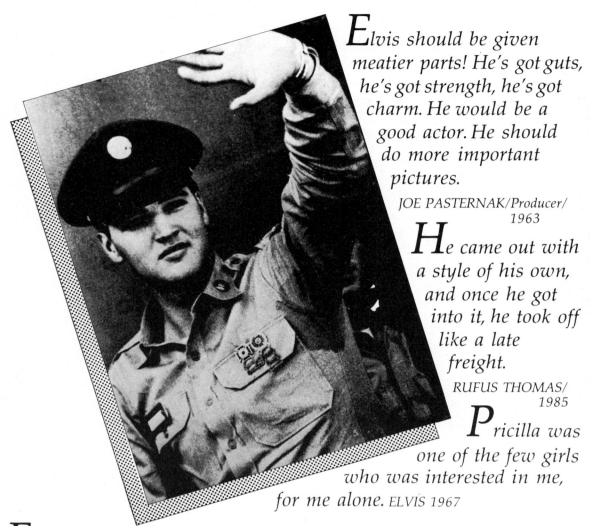

Elvis should be given meatier parts! He's got guts, he's got strength, he's got charm. He would be a good actor. He should do more important pictures.

JOE PASTERNAK/Producer/ 1963

He came out with a style of his own, and once he got into it, he took off like a late freight.

RUFUS THOMAS/ 1985

Pricilla was one of the few girls who was interested in me, for me alone. ELVIS 1967

Elvis was back in the living room and as I walked through the door leading into the living room, Priscilla was behind me ... so I pulled her around beside me and said Elvis this is Priscilla he jumped out of his chair like it was a hot seat! and got real nervous and shaky. I learned two months later why he jumped up so fast that night. It was because he saw Debra Paget in her face immediately, he fell in love with Debra while making 'Love Me Tender'.

CURRIE GRANT/Army Pal

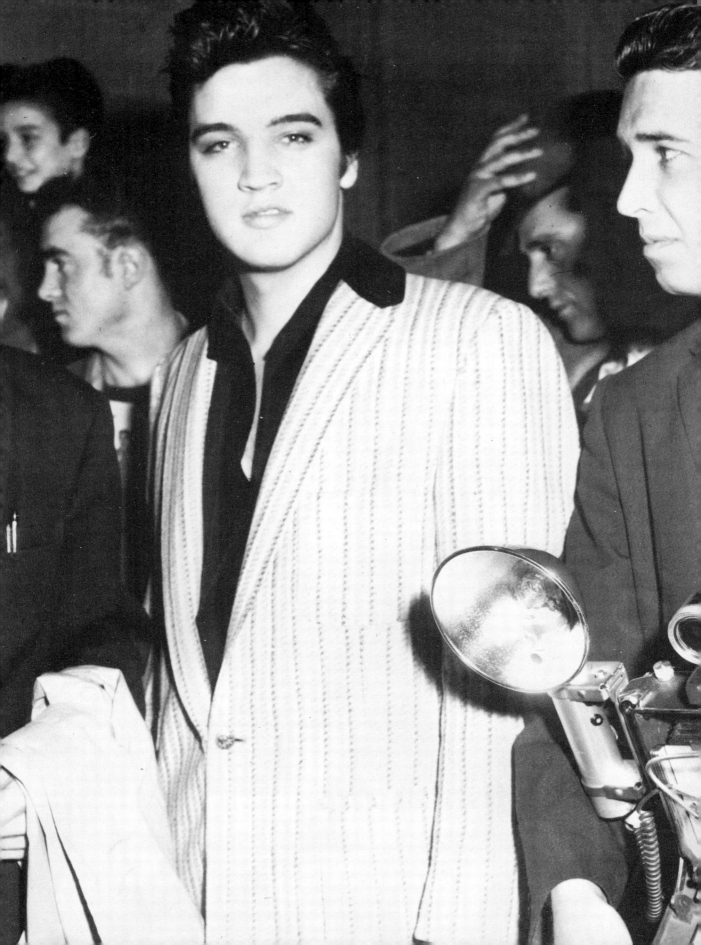

*P*resley is now a highly polished, perfectly timed spectacularly successful show business machine. He performed about twenty numbers with supreme confidence in a routine which was better constructed and choreographed that most Broadway musicals.

Critic "VARIETY"
Madison Square Garden 1972

*H*e had so much energy we had to sit up nights to wear him out so that we could sleep.

SCOTTY MOORE

He's fooled us all, we had our stomach full to here of these celebrities, singers and actors and we figured Presley for just another lightweight. But he's never angled himself into anything easy and he shows exceptionally good judgement for a kid worth a few million dollars. This guy Elvis has made it popular to be a good soldier. It's great for us.
ARMY COMMANDANT/1960

*H*e came down and sat at the dinin' room table, he said where is it? I gave it to him, he slipped it on his finger and looked at it and said, God, won't Sammy Davis Jr. shit a brick when he sees this! How much do I owe ya? I told him $55,000. He said, you gotta be kiddin! No Elvis, it's got an eleven-and-one-half-carat diamond in it. Well all right Elvis smiled, then looked at me with that lopsided grin now I want to do something for you Lowell, what do you want.

LOWELL HAYS/Jewellery Designer

61

*T*here were times when I protested, but in the long run, I was devoted to the man, to do his bidding, and I would do whatever he wanted me to do, whether or not it was good for his health didn't seem to make any difference.

RICK STANLEY/*Stepbrother*

*Y*ou gotta remember one thing, he had been in real pain. He had blood clots in his legs, he had hypoglycemia, he had an extremely enlarged heart, he had glaucoma. He was susceptible to respiratory ailments. His liver was twice normal size plus a twisted colon.

JOHN O'GRADY/*Private Detective*

*W*ith all his high spirits and his rushing about, Elvis is the most relaxed person I know. Often while we were waiting for a scene to be shot he'd pick up his guitar loll on a chair and start to sing and everyone within earshot would fall under his spell.

DOLORES HART/Actress

*H*e touched their lives, the first time I met him, it was like a magnet. I feel he had a special touch from God.

BETH PEASE/Editor/Graceland News

I got a lot of pressure from producers to get him to parties, but he never went, he brought his own party from Memphis with him.

STAN BROSSETTE/Publicist of 11 Presley Pictures

I once tried to get Elvis to make a public appearance against the Colonel's advice, if you can get Elvis to do it the Colonel said, you can have him - Elvis stayed home.

SPYROS SKOURAS/Former Head 20th Century Fox

64

For the four New York shows, Elvis grossed $730,000 and the album sold the predictable million plus copies at six dollars apiece. Elvis got to keep about a third of the concert money and a sixth of the record take. That eventually came to about $1.2 million for six hours of singing.
JOAN DEARY/R.C.A. 1973

My crushing ambition in life was to be as big as Elvis Presley.
JOHN LENNON

Who's my favorite actress?,- Lassie, my favorite actors are Brando, Dean and John Wayne.
ELVIS/1956

He said he wished he could go out and walk down the street like other people, we used to talk about his mother and his childhood. His mother came up in every conversation.
MRS MARIAN COCKE/
Nurse Memphis Baptist Hospital

*E*lvis is a tremendous entertainer, certainly he would have made it without me, but I know that like all good things, too much can be harmful. I make sure Elvis isn't exploited and over-promoted.

COLONEL TOM PARKER

*T*here's so much warmth and charm in him that you can't possibly feel from any distance, it's when you're close to him that the real message comes through and you really begin to understand him.

MYRNA SMITH/Singer Sweet Inspirations

*A*ny girl who wants to date Presley knows she has to get along with his boys.

JOAN BLACKMAN/Co Star Blue Hawii

*E*lvis must have been about 20 and Natalie Wood was 18, I'd have about 20 people over and those two would sit there and neck all evening! Elvis was just mad about her.

SHELLEY WINTERS/Actress

On one occasion he gave me a Harley-Davidson motor cycle, I said I could hardly sit on the thing let along ride it. He rented about 15 miles of motorway outside Los Angeles the next day, so that I could ride it in a straight line.

SUZANNA LEIGH/Actress

I'd rather die on stage than in bed.

ELVIS 1971

One night, I'll never forget. A woman ran down front to the stage and Elvis leaned over to kiss her, she had a golden crown on a small pillow, he asked her What's this? She told him It's for you, you're the King! He told her No honey! Christ is the King, I'm just a singer.

J.D. SUMNER/Gospel Singer

There have been many accolades uttered about his talent and performances through the years all of which I agree with wholeheartedly, I shall miss him dearly as a friend.

FRANK SINATRA/1977

I would like to be able to take my daughter to a carnival or a movie without being mobbed.
ELVIS

*M*y mother was watching the Ed Sullivan Show and Elvis came on. I went out and got a guitar right away, but I couldn't play it, I was too small, but that was the start.

BRUCE SPRINGSTEEN/Rock Singer

*B*ack then people would laugh at his sideburns and his pink coat and call him a sissy - he had a pretty hard road to go. In some areas, motorcycle gangs would come to the shows. They would come to get Elvis, but he never worried about it, he went right out and did his thing and before the show was over, they were standing in line to get his autograph too.

CARL PERKINS/U.S.A. Rock and Roll Star

*A*ll the arrangements were worked out in the studio, and everything was spontaneous. Today everybody makes records like that but back then, Elvis was the only one.

BONES HOWE/Record
Producer

A lot of people are knocking this Elvis Presley guy, why I think he's all right.

BURL IVES

*E*lvis is the greatest talent this country, maybe the world, has ever produced.

Gov. RAY BLANTON/
Tennessee

Elvis Presley came to my Deek Lake training camp. He told me he didn't want nobody to bother us, he wanted peace and quiet. I don't admire nobody, but Elvis Presley was the sweetest, most humble and nicest man you'd ever meet.

MUHAMMAD ALI

He was one hell of a guy, he'd always remember you by name, he'd grab a handful of dinner rolls and play touch football with the guards as we escorted him to his suite from the showroom, sometimes he carried a bible and would quote passages by heart.

MIKE ALBRECH/Security Guard/Hilton Hotel

A minute after the record was finished, the phones began ringing and I called for that cotton-pickin' Elvis to get right on over to the station, but he was hiding in a movie, afraid the kids would laugh at him.

DEWEY PHILLIPS/
First DJ to play an Elvis record

Elvis sits around with us and jokes just like one of us, and when he asks me to do anything, he always calls me mister. Why you would think he was working for us instead of the other way round.
BIG BARNIE SMITH/Graceland Guard

He invited me over to his place after a day filming **Wild In The Country***. I said yes and he said Joe would pick me up at 8 o'clock. It was as close to a relaxed family evening as possible. We all just sat around and played card games. Elvis was a friendly host, he made me feel at home.*
CHRISTINA CRAWFORD/Joan Crawford's Daughter

What kept him going is that he wanted to continue being Elvis Presley.
MARTY LACKER/Former Elvis aide

The first record I heard of his was "Mystery Train" and I knew that was it.
CONWAY TWITTY/Singer

The hit parade should start at No. 2. Elvis has that number 1 slot reserved.
HANK MARVIN/Guitarist 1960

The rock world has lost its figurehead.
DAVID ESSEX/August 17th, 1977

Elvis is the Pied Piper of rock'n'roll, a swivel hipped, leg-lashing entertainment bomb who blasted the downtown area into chaos all day yesterday. Screaming, fainting teenagers lined the streets early to catch a glimpse of Elvis, a rockabilly, gyrating singer whose sexy, sultry style has caused a revolution.

THE EVENING INDEPENDENT/Florida 1956

I think there's a big difference between thrill driving and just pressing a motor to it's biggest strength. That's where Jimmy Dean made his fatal mistake. He was driving himself, challenging himself—not the car. I don't worry about me. I don't like suicide.

ELVIS

He's the total man.

KANG RHEE/Karate Instructor

This cat came out . . . he had this sneer on his face and he stood behind the mike for five minutes, I'll bet, before he made a move. Then he started to move his hips real slow . . . he made chills run up my back, man.

BOB LUMAN/Country Artist

Our friendship goes back to before he did his first television show, I felt sorry for the man. I don't think he lived two years as himself. Maybe he was too protected, who is to say.
PERRY COMO/1977

It started off with Elvis buying Priscilla a horse. Now she didn't have anyone to ride with, so Elvis brought his cousin Patsy Presley a horse so she could ride with her. Then he brought himself one and when he saw us looking on forlornly at them riding horses, he decided we all should have horses. He brought everyone of us a horse.
RED WEST

I think that part of America died when Presley passed away, he was accepted like the Empire State Building, the statue of Liberty. Elvis Presley - he was America man.

CARL PERKINS

One day on the set of Spinout, I asked Elvis why he was so quiet. He said I've learned to live with loneliness.

SANDY DAVIS/Journalist/Photo Screen/1966

Elvis had the power over people's imaginations that would enable him to obtain high office.

RICHARD NIXON/
Ex. U.S. President

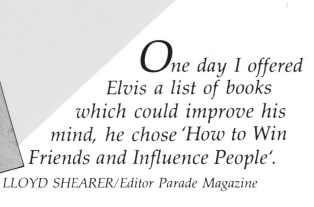

One day I offered Elvis a list of books which could improve his mind, he chose 'How to Win Friends and Influence People'.

LLOYD SHEARER/Editor Parade Magazine

*He was good. He never had to take a back seat to anybody. I thought **Don't Be Cruel** was one of the greatest songs I ever heard.*

JERRY LEE LEWIS/1985

I loved the man as a brother, and the impact he had on music will never be forgotten because he taught white America to get down.
JAMES BROWN

*M*oney is meant to be spread around, the more happiness it helps create, the more it's worth.
ELVIS

*W*hen R.C.A. asked me to take pictures of a man called Elvis, I was told I had better not use colour film. Use black and white he might not last longer than six months.
ALFRED WERTHEIMER

*D*eath was due to a severely irregular heart-beat possibly caused by high blood pressure and artery disease.
DR. JERRY FRANCISCO

*W*hile I was in Hollywood, I actually saw Elvis Presley, we were driving along and this big white Cadillac pulled up alongside us at a stop light. There he was, I thought I would die. He was sitting inside and there were some other men with him all dressed in black. He's a terribly good looking man, I couldn't take my eyes off him, then the light changed and that was the end of it.
HAYLEY MILLS/British Actress

A truly good man who never forgot his friends or his fans.
LIBERACE

I think Elvis Presley is going to be the one who will be the great popular entertainer of his generation. I think he must be well managed and pretty interesting himself.
MAURICE CHEVALIER

I had never met before or since any man who could so totally disarm you with charm, generosity and what appeared to be spontaneous love, as could Elvis Presley.
DAVE HEBLER/Bodyguard

*H*e had so much energy in those days, every day, every night was the same. He chewed his fingernails, drummed his hands against his thighs, tapped his feet and every chance he got, he'd start combing his hair.
SCOTTY MOORE/1966

*W*hen happy folk laugh in the sun
And all around's serene,
Just when she's least expecting it,
It's then what might have been
Comes back to pierce her heart a new
Life's golden hours hold sorrow, too.
THE FRIENDSHIP BOOK/Tuesday August 16th 1977

If you were a teenager in the late 1950's, you owed something to Elvis Presley, his unfettered singing style freed you from something you didn't even know confined you, when you listened to his records or danced to them, you felt you could breathe, as though all the nameless oppression would eventually go away.

JOE WARD/Music Writer

There was nothing morally reprehensible about Elvis's performance it was merely awful.

NEW YORK TIMES/ On Frank Sinatra T.V. Show with Elvis

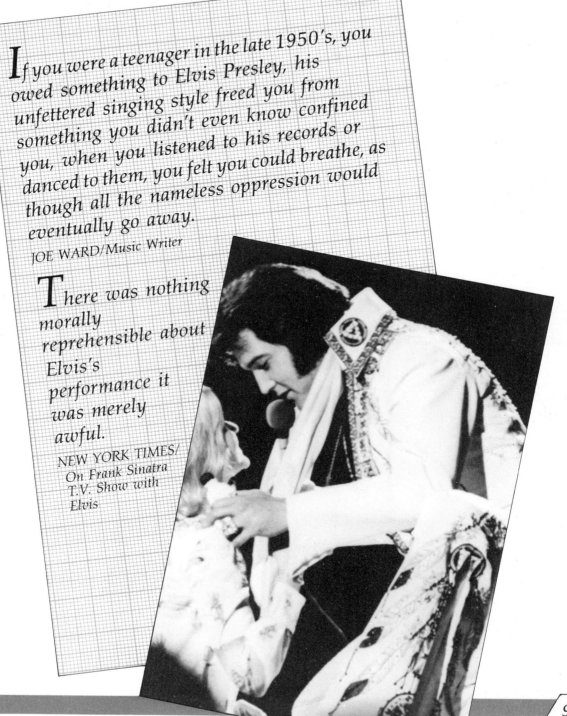

*W*ell we're definitely grown up now. If he's dead then we can't be kids anymore, the effect of his lifetime is well marked.
PAUL SIMON/1977

*E*veryone in rock'n'roll including myself was touched by his spirit, I was, and always will be a fan.
BRYAN FERRY/Roxy Music

*O*nce I asked him what he wanted to be, and he scratched his head and said, the only thing I really want to do is sing. He wasn't a top student, but he made it without worrying me.
MISS MILDRED SCRIVENER/
12th Grade Teacher

I told him after his appearance, he should go back to driving trucks.
JIM DENNY/Manager Grand Ole Opry 1955

I made a bargain with him at the outset I don't try to sing and he don't interfere with the deals.
COLONEL TOM PARKER

I wouldn't let my daughter walk across the street to see Elvis Presley perform.
BILLY GRAHAM/Evangelist 1955

O ne of the things I most respected in Elvis was the fact that he never forgot that he was a man who came from good and humble people.
BURT REYNOLDS/Actor

N obody who plays this town is in the same league as Presley as far as impact is concerned, room occupancy goes up all over the city whenever he is in town.
DICK LANE/Entertainment Director/
  Las Vegas Hilton

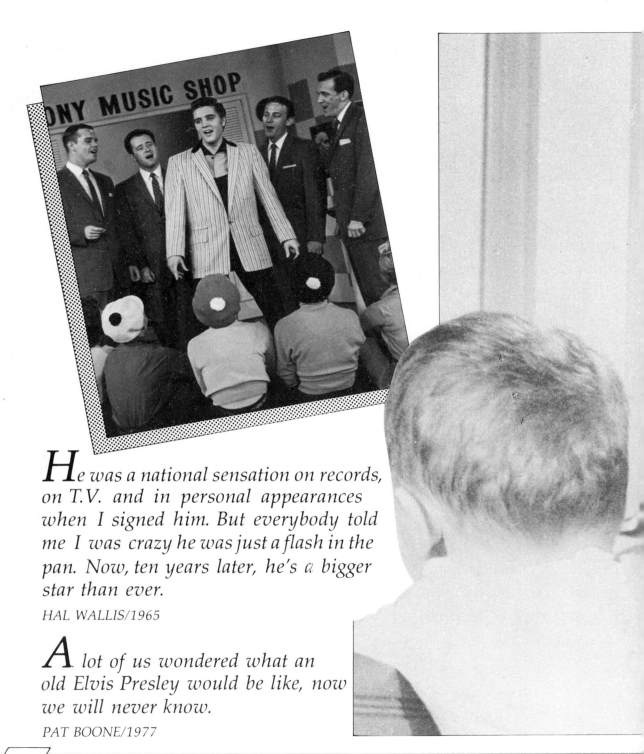

*H*e was a national sensation on records, on T.V. and in personal appearances when I signed him. But everybody told me I was crazy he was just a flash in the pan. Now, ten years later, he's a bigger star than ever.

HAL WALLIS/1965

A lot of us wondered what an old Elvis Presley would be like, now we will never know.

PAT BOONE/1977

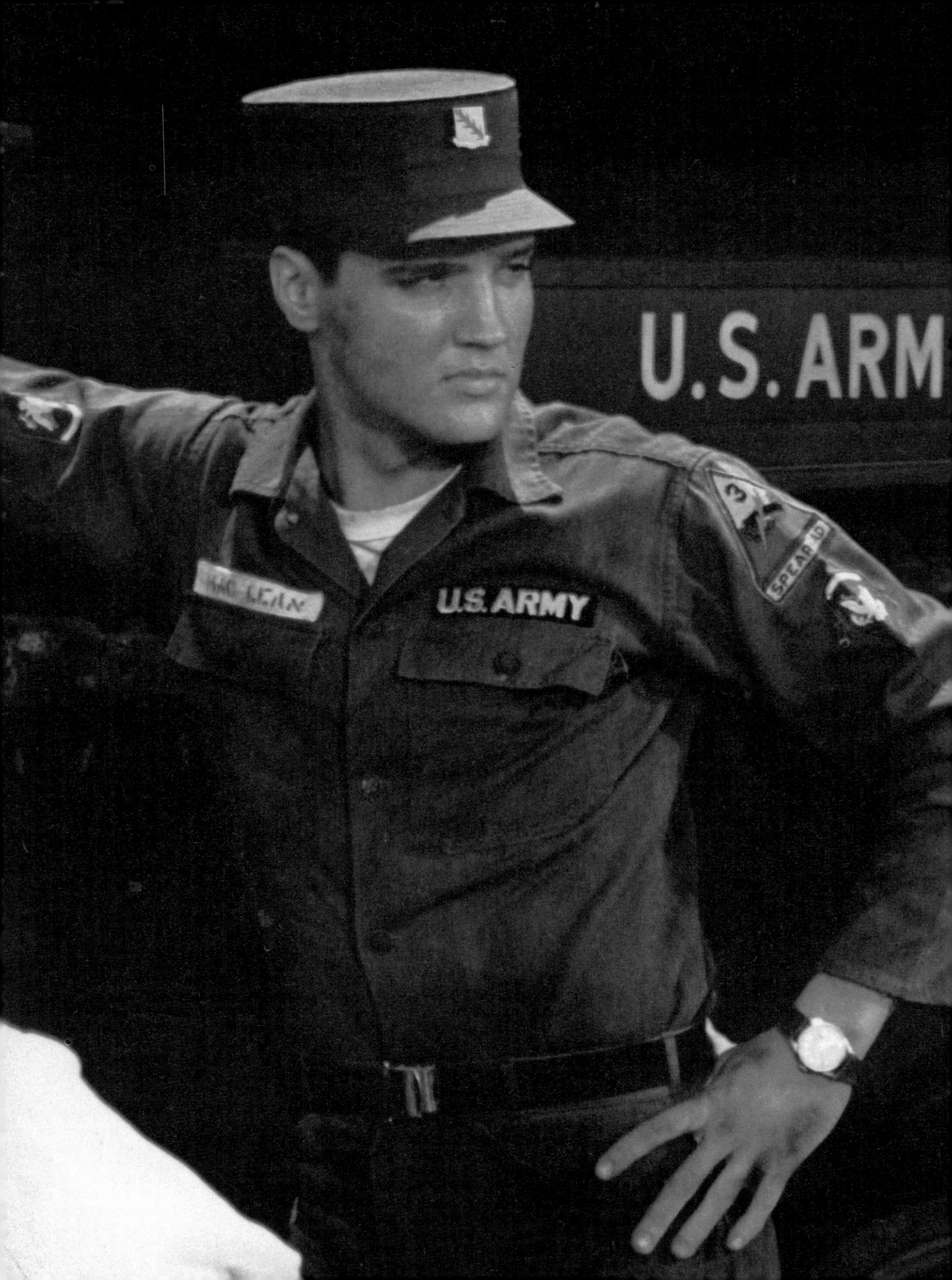
U.S. ARM
U.S. ARMY

*H*e is a brilliant performer a mammoth figure in pop history. His timing is superb, his sense of line and form in his movement is superb, one day someone will actually put Elvis into a good movie, but they better do it quick before it's too late.
BRIDGET BYRNE/
    Los Angeles Herald/1970

I wasn't exactly a James Bond in the movie **Double Trouble**, but then, no one ever asked Sean Connery to sing a song while dodging bullets.
ELVIS

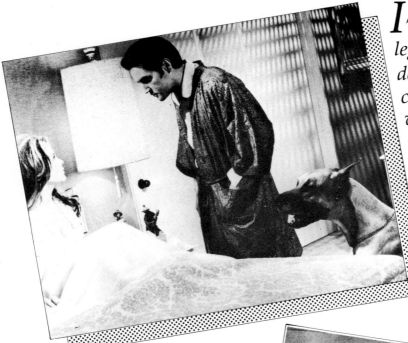

I've written on arms, legs, ankles - any place decent where people can take soap and wash it off. I don't want no daddy with a shotgun after me.

ELVIS

We have a lot of fun on a date and our relationship could not be called anything but the casual, happy companionship between a boy and a girl, if you try to make anything more than that of it you will be wrong.

JULIET PROWSE 1960

Elvis may be gone, but the echo will never die.

CASEY KASEM/U.S. T.V. Presenter

I have no need of bodyguards, but I have very special and specific uses for two highly trained certified accountants, an expert transportation man to handle travel arrangements, make reservations, take care of luggage, etc. A wardrobe man and a confidential aide and a security man who will handle safety arrangements in large cities where crowds of people are involved more than that, they are just my friends.

ELVIS

Elvis was a voracious reader and whether it was football, singing or reading, if Elvis got enthusiastic about it he was bent on becoming an expert. I honestly believe Elvis could debate a Harvard Professor on the subjects he was interested in.

ALAN FORTAS/Elvis Associate

I was tame to what they do now, all I did was jiggle.

ELVIS/1974

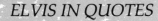

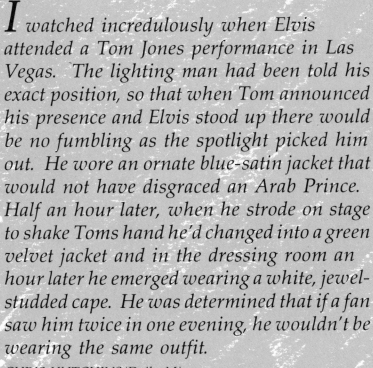

I watched incredulously when Elvis attended a Tom Jones performance in Las Vegas. The lighting man had been told his exact position, so that when Tom announced his presence and Elvis stood up there would be no fumbling as the spotlight picked him out. He wore an ornate blue-satin jacket that would not have disgraced an Arab Prince. Half an hour later, when he strode on stage to shake Toms hand he'd changed into a green velvet jacket and in the dressing room an hour later he emerged wearing a white, jewel-studded cape. He was determined that if a fan saw him twice in one evening, he wouldn't be wearing the same outfit.

CHRIS HUTCHINS/*Daily Mirror*

I was watching a clip of "Loving You" and my dad saw the expression on my face, looked at the screen and said, son now I know what you mean.

BILLY BREMNER/*Guitarist Rockpile*

Life was pretty good, all except them last years. Then it got so I don't think he had a peaceful day. I'd see him and say, How you doin' son, and he'd say to me, "Not so good, Uncle Vester, I can't seem to catch my damn breath."

VESTER PRESELY

*E*lvis was probably the sweetest, kindest man who ever lived, but ultimately, he was trapped behind the fences of his home because everyone he met wanted something from him.

BOB GREENE/Writer/The Nashville Banner

*T*here was one time, back when we were riding horses a lot that he brought his horse, Sun, through the back door at Graceland and paraded around on him in the den, imagine if you had guests in your home and you came riding through the living room on a horse. It would blow their minds.

CHARLIE HODGE

Eventually, I just got tired of singing to turtles and the guys I'd just beaten up.

ELVIS

Since his arrival, Presley had demonstrated leadership ability and proved himself worthy of promotion to sergeant.

Capt. HUBERT CHILDRESS/Company Commander

All I know is that our personal relationship was just that - very personal and very special. Its true that at one point we discussed marriage, but we were both very young and for whatever reasons, it didn't work out.

ANN-MARGRET/Actress

You know, I think it's entirely possible to die of a broken heart . . . and I think that was a contributing factor.

SAM PHILLIPS

I actually met Elvis, for the first time when I was five at the Tennessee fairgrounds. He patted my head, I remembered it but he didn't.

GINGER ALDEN/Last Girlfriend

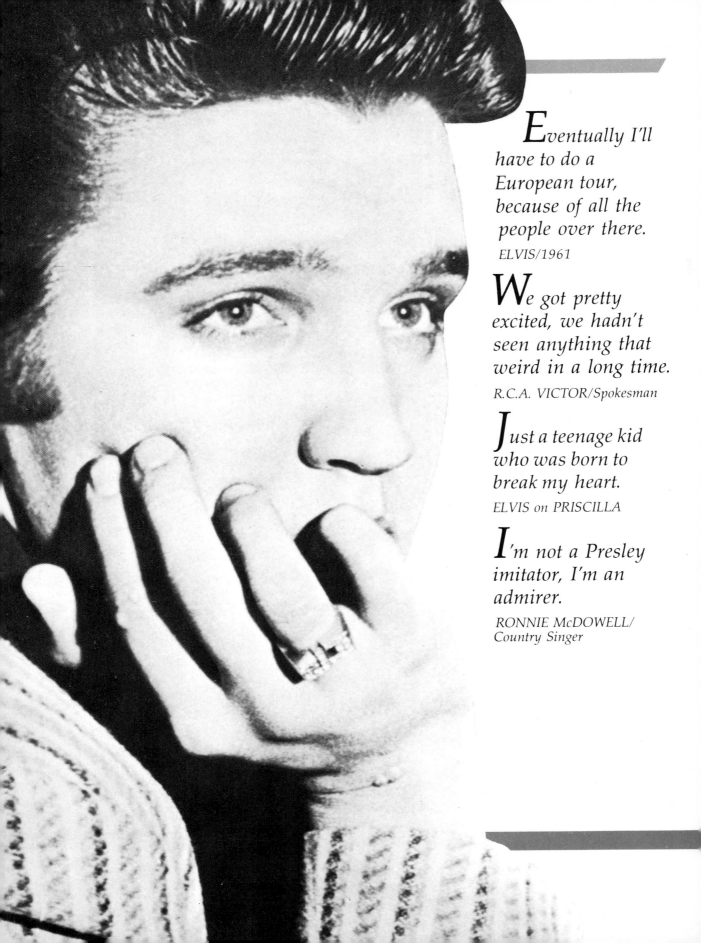

Eventually I'll have to do a European tour, because of all the people over there.
ELVIS/1961

We got pretty excited, we hadn't seen anything that weird in a long time.
R.C.A. VICTOR/Spokesman

Just a teenage kid who was born to break my heart.
ELVIS on PRISCILLA

I'm not a Presley imitator, I'm an admirer.
RONNIE McDOWELL/Country Singer

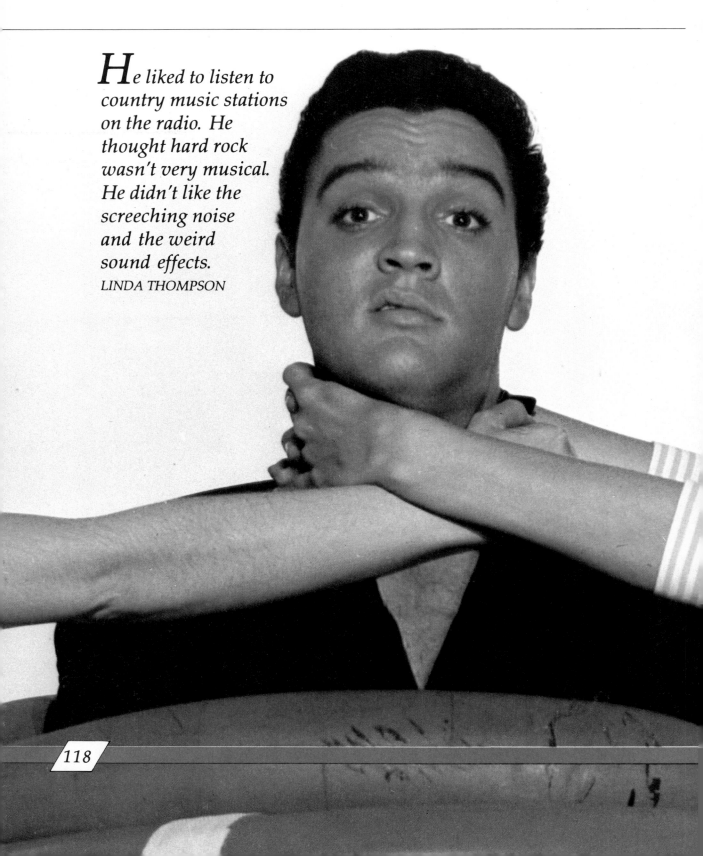

He liked to listen to country music stations on the radio. He thought hard rock wasn't very musical. He didn't like the screeching noise and the weird sound effects.
LINDA THOMPSON

We were all in his hotel suite, it was so damned awkward. Elvis disappeared after a while into the bedroom with a bunch of the girls. Karen and I were talking outside with Elvis's date and Karen was confused. Elvis's date said, "Elvis is only reading the bible to them" We snuck up to the door and watched and that's what he was doing.

FRANK LIEBERMAN/*Journalist*

119

I talked to Elvis about three months before he died, he said I'm bored, so bored and the only time I feel alive, really alive, is when I'm in front of my audience, my people! Thats the only time that I really feel like I'm human.

BARBARA PITTMAN/U.S. Singer

*H*e had the first pink Cadillac I'd ever seen: pink and black. It has air conditioning, but Elvis drove all over with the windows rolled down.

WANDA JACKSON/1955

I applaud the parents of teenagers who work to get the blood and horror gangster stories off T.V. They should work harder against the new alleged singer, Elvis Presley.

HEDDA HOPPER/1957

*S*ometimes when I walk into a room at home and see all those gold records hanging around the walls, I think they must belong to another person, not me, I just can't believe that it's me.

ELVIS

*J*ust a day or so before Elvis died, I told him, I keep hearing you going to announce your engagement. When are you going to get married? Only God knows, he said. I got a feeling that maybe he was changing his mind.

VERNON PRESLEY/1978

*H*e doesn't want to entertain, we've asked him and he said, I'd rather not sir. General Van Natta said he just wants to mind his own business, do his job and be left alone. He's a good soldier.

Maj. Gen. THOMAS F. VAN NATTA/Commanding General 3rd Armored Division

*I*n death as in life, Elvis has kept the cash registers ringing, at the end ironically enough, as popular as that song was, he wasn't doing it "His Way" at all. The incredible fact is, however, Elvis remains as alive today as he ever was.

DAVID FROST/British T.V. Personality/1979.

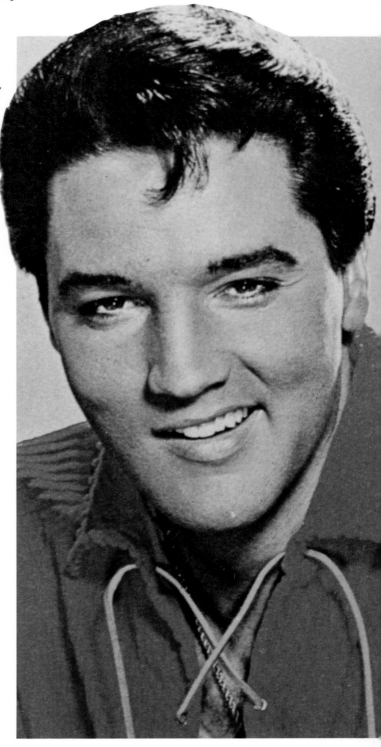

I guess over the years I've drawn more than 10,000 pictures of Elvis, I never got tired of drawing him, because he changed so much, he never seemed to look the same.

BETTY HARPER/Artist

Elvis Presley moved his tongue and indulged in wordless so-called singing on the Sullivan show, which at best was simply in very bad taste.

Reverend WILLIAM J. SHANNON/Catholic Sun 1956

If there was going to be company, the first thing Elvis would do was to hide the peanut butter. He just loved peanut butter and was afraid the company would eat all of it.

BILLY SMITH/Elvis First Cousin and Closest Friend

He could always talk to people, and he was never shy. He had a way of getting along with others, and he'd go out of his way to avoid trouble. If one of his friends got mad, he'd give him his toys to try to get the other fellows happy again.

VERNON PRESLEY/1954

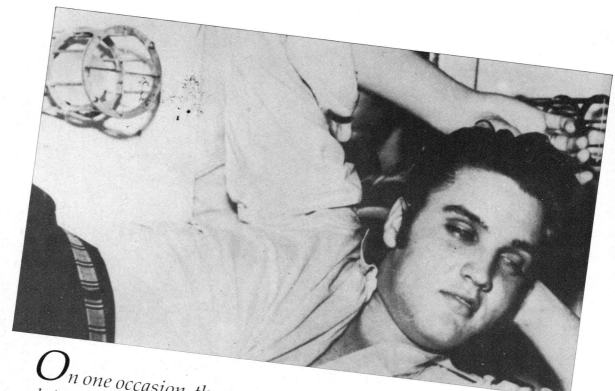

*O*n one occasion, there was a little boy, six or seven years old, he was dying of cancer, and he wanted a letter from Elvis before he went. Elvis just didn't send the boy a letter, he went to visit him, two or three times, and brought him presents, I don't know of a single instance of genuine need which he heard about when he failed to do something. He was an incredibly caring person.

HENRY LOEB/Mayor of Memphis/1960-63

I loved Paris. I didn't have to sign too many autographs, and I became an ordinary guy for a while.

ELVIS

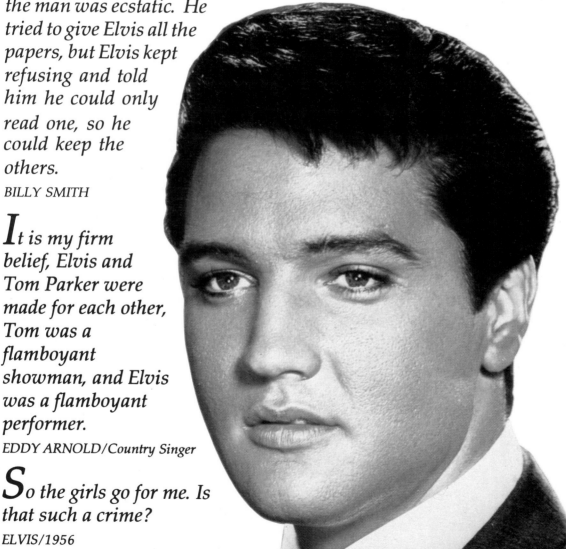

*B*ack when the money first started really rolling in, Elvis was really happy, he wanted everyone to share his happiness with him. That was Elvis. I remember one time in Memphis, when Elvis wanted a newspaper, he went up to a stand and told the vendor he wanted a paper. Elvis pulled out a $100 bill and the man said, I don't have the change for anything that big, Elvis said Well, then just keep the change, the man was ecstatic. He tried to give Elvis all the papers, but Elvis kept refusing and told him he could only read one, so he could keep the others.

BILLY SMITH

*I*t is my firm belief, Elvis and Tom Parker were made for each other, Tom was a flamboyant showman, and Elvis was a flamboyant performer.

EDDY ARNOLD/Country Singer

*S*o the girls go for me. Is that such a crime?

ELVIS/1956

*E*lvis who was born on Jan 8th 1935 had a double critical day on August 15. His intellectual and physical cycles crossed at a critically low point. He was also low emotionally on the day of his death, Elvis was on a triple low. All three cycles intersected at a low point, he was as depressed as he could possibly be.

BERNARD GITTELSON/Author/Biorythm Forecasting

I spent four days as his guest at the International Hotel in Las Vegas, I offered him $500,000 for two performances - one at Wembley and one at the Royal Festival Hall for charity. Funnily enough it wasn't the money that caused problems it was his fear of flying and worry about security.

JEFFREY ARCHER/British Politician and Best-Selling Author

*H*e's a champion who has lived and kept the title he's for real. Elvis is a southern child that is down to earth, he's beautiful, just beautiful. I saw Elvis not long ago, when I was singing on stage, I was singing I Can't Stop Loving You and I heard someone yelling and clapping and I looked and I saw Elvis waving to me, he is true, a real pioneer.

LITTLE RICHARD/Singer

*E*lvis Presley is probably the main founding father of rock music. He was an unheralded genius despite his fame as a singer. Yes, he was the genius behind a new music that changed western civilization for all time.

PETER NOONE/Herman's Hermits

*E*lvis was much like his father. Both men were able to project tremendous strength and confidence, but lurking beneath their fortitude was always a profound sense of insecurity.

BILLY STANLEY/Step Brother

I find Elvis Presley unfit for family audiences.

ED SULLIVAN/U.S. T.V. Host 1955

135

You can live ten lifetimes and you'll never find another like him. He's got a heart of gold, He'll give you the shirt off his back.
RICHARD DAVIS/Close Friend

If I slept with every woman they (the movie mags) say I have, I would have been dead a long time ago.
ELVIS/1966

The one thing I bought as a star that meant the most to me was a $50 picture of Jesus I gave my parents.
ELVIS

Before he could sing the first song, the audience would give him a ten minute standing ovation.
MARTY LACKER

Outside of Walt Disney, Elvis is the only sure thing in this business.
BEN SCHWALB/Film
            Producer
            Tickle Me

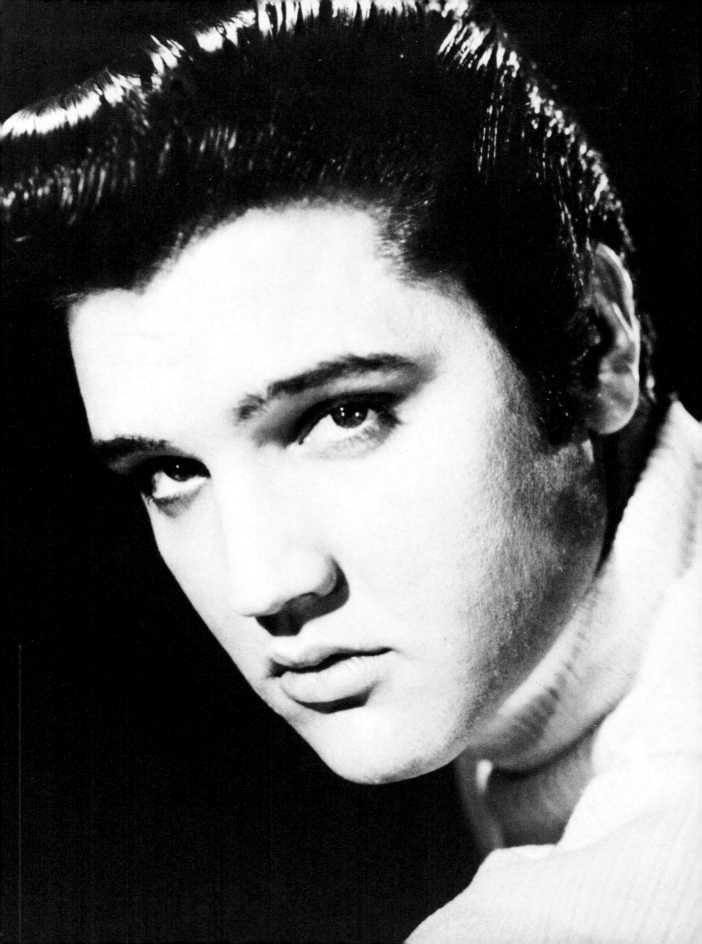

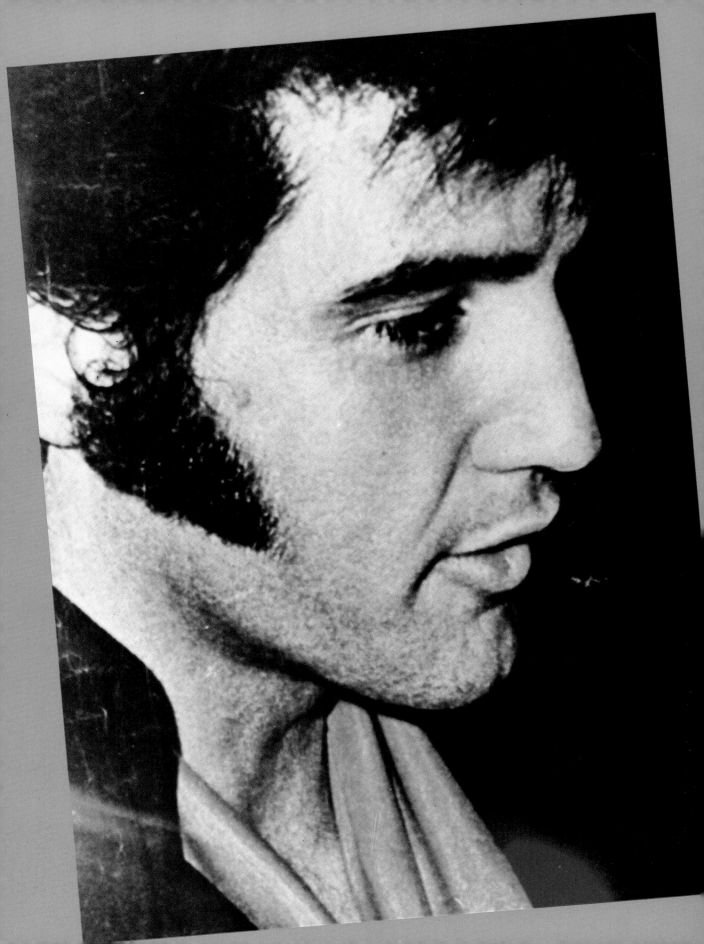

*Y*eah, he was a crazy sonofagun and yeah, we had lots of fights. But I loved the sonofagun. There were times I hugged that guy like a little baby. Because let me tell you, when he died at 42, he was still a little baby, a spoiled, lovable kid.

RED WEST/*Bodyguard*

I look nothing like him but when I was playing the role, people behaved as if they really wanted me to be Elvis – as if they really wanted him to still be alive.

KURT RUSSEL/*Actor* 'Elvis The Movie'

*E*lvis Presley was my greatest influence.

KYU SAKAMOTO/*Japanese Singer*

*W*hen I got married, Elvis had brought me a small wedding gift, I had no idea until I came out of the church, there was a brand new car. I drove to church in a Volkswagen and left in a Mercury Marquis.

DICK GROB/*Bodyguard*

I could not imagine that guy dying, he was so incredibly important to me, to go on and do what I want to do, when I heard the news, it was like somebody took a piece out of me, he was an artist and he was into being an artist. On stage he encompassed everything - he was laughing at the world, and he was laughing at himself, but at the same time he was dead serious.

BRUCE SPINGSTEEN

The problem is that Elvis did not simply change musical history, though of course he did that, he changed history, pure and simple, and in doing so he became history. If any individual of our time can be said to have changed the world, Elvis Presley is the one.
GREIL MARCUS/Rock Author

I believe I will see Elvis in heaven.
BILLY GRAHAM/Evangelist/1978

Elvis is about the nicest guy ever, I think I'd like to marry him.
TUESDAY WELD/Co Star, **Wild in Country**

His one speciality is an accentuated movement of the body that here-to-fore has been primarily identified with the repertoire of the blonde bombshells of the burlesque runway.
THE NEW YORK TIMES

W hen he came to make a record, he said it
was just a demo for his mother. I realized he
was really auditioning for me, but was too
shy to come right out and say so.
SAM PHILLIPS/Co. Owner Sun Records

*E*lvis presents a fascinating question, some call him the devil incarnate, others declare he is the next thing to God. Who was he?. I predict Elvis will be the first entertainer whose life will be seriously studied by historians.

DR. JOHN BAKKE/Memphis State University's Theatre and Communiation Arts Department.

I consider it my patriotic duty, to keep Elvis in the 90% tax bracket while he's in the army.

COLONEL PARKER/1959

There are several unbelievable things about Elvis, but the most incredible is his staying power in a world where meteoric careers fade like shooting stars.
NEWSWEEK

I adored Elvis, I must say I prefer early Elvis to post army Elvis. I thought at first he was black. When I heard Heartbreak Hotel. I thought it was really jazzy.
GEORGE MELLY/Jazzman/1985

I'm 1-A in the draft, I'll go when I have to of course, but I would like a little more time the way things are. It'll be quite a drop from $10,000 a week to $74 a month.

ELVIS/1956

People put him in a place he couldn't live up to, they just didn't understand that he wasn't a god, he was a man.

PRISCILLA PRESLEY/Wife

You know he's a real nice friendly fellow.

BUDDY HOLLY

Security was the first thing we'd take all the rooms on the floor. Room service would be told to deliver food to the elevator or to his door, but never go into Elvis's room. Then we prepared Elvis's room. That meant blacking out all the windows of Elvis's bedroom with aluminium foil. Elvis was a nocturnal person and this was to keep out the light so he could sleep the next day. It meant checking the air conditioning, to make sure it worked, because Elvis liked it cold. Cold and dark.

JERRY SCHILLING/Elvis Pr. Officer

He's a great singer. Gosh, he's so great, you have no idea how great he is, really you don't. You have absolutely no comprehension it's absolutely impossible, I can't tell you why he's so great, but he is.

PHIL SPECTOR/Record Producer 1969

He is quite certain that one day he will do some shows in England. Obviously, every member of the public is not an Elvis fan, but everybody must accept that one single man to pull all that love and feeling must have something.
JIMMY SAVILE/British DJ/1960

I suppose it might have been different if my brother had lived, a lot of things might have been different. But he didn't live and I grew up alone. I guess my mother -and my father too, of course were trying to make up for that, by giving me enough love for two.
ELVIS

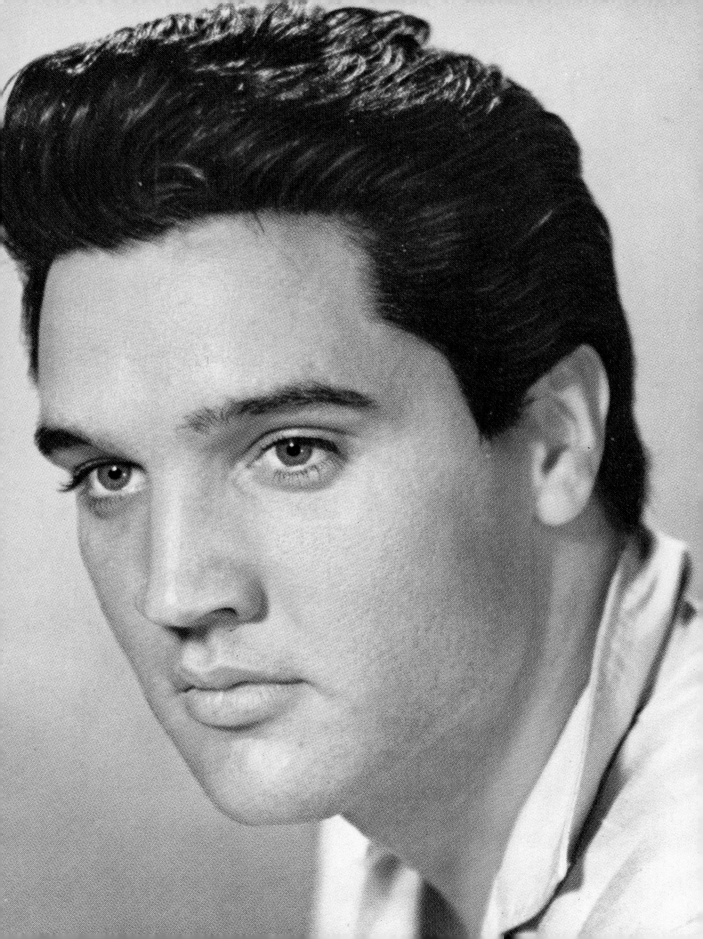

I've got a ridiculously soft spot for Elvis, if anybody is the King it's him, I don't know why, but there's something in his voice that grabs me.

IRENE HANDL/British Comedienne 1970

I was just a star-struck fan, I climbed over the wall in Audubon Drive and I never left.

LAMAR FIKE/1976

Its time to remind those who are not his greatest fans that the biggest part of Elvis Presley is his heart, it is full of love for everyone.

DANNY THOMAS

Elvis is suffering from itchy underwear and hot shoes.

LAS VEGAS
COLUMNIST

*A*fter seeing Elvis perform in Lubbock, Texas in 1954, I wrote my first tune. It's funny how things work out, I mean, Elvis is now recording my songs.

MAC DAVIS/Songwriter

*H*e can't sing a lick, and makes up for vocal shortcomings with the weirdest and plainly planned suggestive animation, short of an Aborigine's mating dance.

JACK O'BRIEN/1955 Writer

*W*e sometimes flew from Memphis to Dallas just to get a hamburger, Elvis was convinced that Dallas was the only town that could make a decent hamburger.

NIGEL WINFIELD/ Pilot, Convair Jet

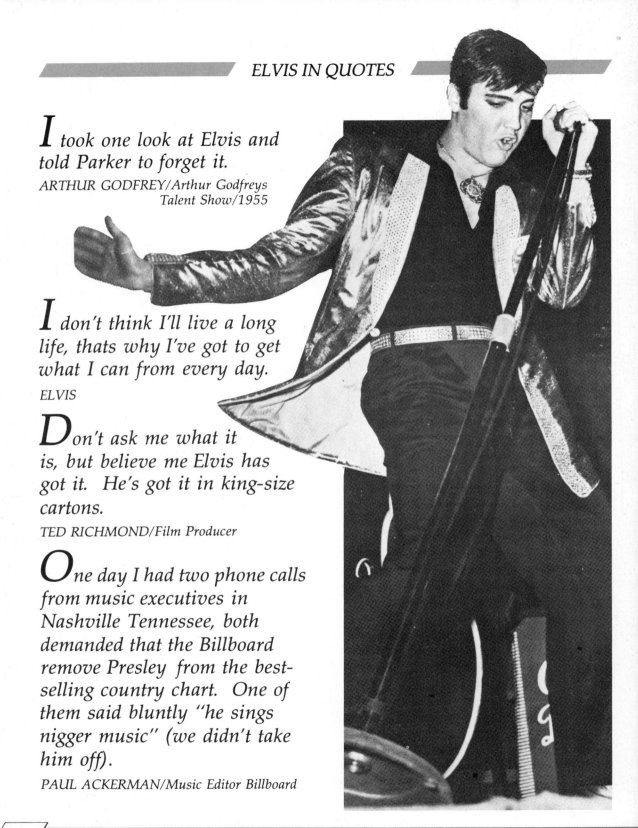

I took one look at Elvis and told Parker to forget it.
ARTHUR GODFREY/Arthur Godfreys Talent Show/1955

I don't think I'll live a long life, thats why I've got to get what I can from every day.
ELVIS

*D*on't ask me what it is, but believe me Elvis has got it. He's got it in king-size cartons.
TED RICHMOND/Film Producer

*O*ne day I had two phone calls from music executives in Nashville Tennessee, both demanded that the Billboard remove Presley from the best-selling country chart. One of them said bluntly "he sings nigger music" (we didn't take him off).
PAUL ACKERMAN/Music Editor Billboard

I don't know a lot
about music, in my
line I don't have to.
ELVIS

He was the one that started everything rolling, and music as we know it today, stems from what Elvis did.
MICKEY GILLEY

He needed and wanted more love than anyone I've ever met he was a super romantic.
LINDA THOMPSON

He didn't even get himself a glass of water, somebody would always have a glass of water ready whenever he needed it.
PATSY LACKER

I don't care if I don't make any money as long as I give them a good show.
ELVIS

Of all his girls, I think Linda Thompson was the best for him.
VERNON PRESLEY

I was near petrified the first time I performed for a really big audience. I wanted to loosen up my voice, so I did the usual - I wiggled my body. Well, believe it or not, only my lower half would wiggle! A fortunate accident, as it turned out.

ELVIS

In almost every city where Elvis appeared, he was given one tribute, or another, what he cherished most however were the official police badges. His collection probably the largest private collection ever, was extremely important to him and heaven help the man who left them behind.
DICK GROB/
Personal Assistant

Whereas Elvis Presley was an inspiration to all by showing that through hard work and dedication we can make the world a better place in which to live; and whereas Elvis Presley's sudden and untimely death truly shocked and saddened the world on August 16, 1977. Now therefore I, Lamar Alexander, as Governor of the State of Tennessee, do hereby proclaim August 16 1979 as Elvis Presley Day.

LAMAR ALEXANDER/Governor/Tennessee/April 10th 1979.

The first time we met was at a record shop in Cleveland, where Elvis was my supporting act. Which was the only time that happened. I never again wanted to follow Elvis. I was very glad I had this big hit record going for me, so that when I came on stage it wasn't totally anticlimatic.

PAT BOONE

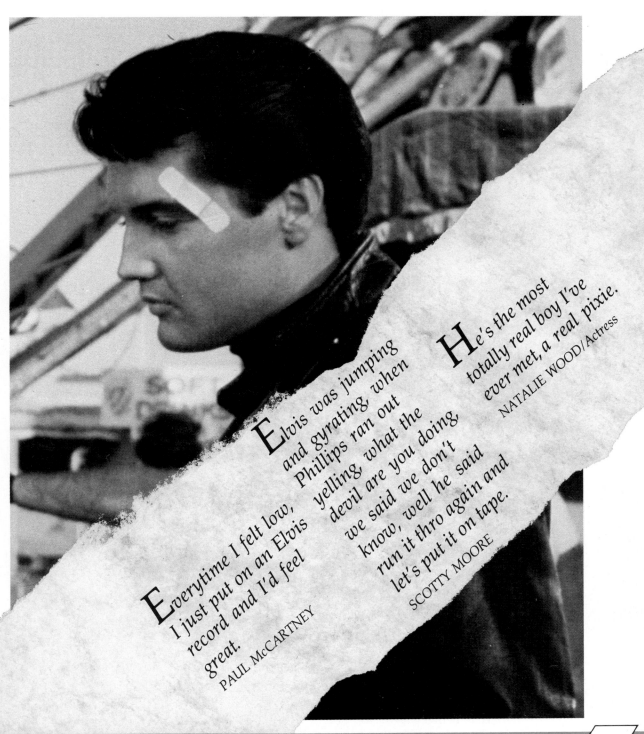

He's the most totally real boy I've ever met, a real pixie.

NATALIE WOOD/Actress

Elvis was jumping and gyrating, when Phillips ran out yelling, what the devil are you doing we said we don't know, well he said run it thro again and let's put it on tape.

SCOTTY MOORE

Everytime I felt low, I just put on an Elvis record and I'd feel great.

PAUL McCARTNEY

*O*nce he began to cry during a concert. It was during a show in Vegas in 1972. He had divorced Priscilla, and she had turned up at the packed show with a girlfriend. He spotted her in the audience, walked over to her and began to sing a romantic song and then he began to weep and the tears ran down his cheeks.

SEAN SHAVER/Photographer

*D*iscount the commercial rubbish he has done often during his career. I just like to think of his trail - blazing glorious best, when he sang black man's music in white style, and taught the world something about true originality. He's still a hero of mine. You don't forget the early influences.

ERIC CLAPTON/British Guitarist

*O*ne of the greatest moments of my life comes when Lisa looks up and smiles just for me.

ELVIS

*W*hat spurred me on to try for success in pop was Elvis. I'd stand for hours in front of a mirror, holding a tennis racquet and pretending I was him. All his movements, the sneer, the pout even his hairstyle.

ALVIN STARDUST/British Singer

It was only a touch football, sure. But it was the roughest, toughest touch football I ever saw. Elvis could have broken his leg or had his teeth knocked out, or his face flattened, if Col. Tom Parker could have seen it he would have cried like a baby, there was a million dollars' worth of Elvis Presley running around out there, acting like he didn't have a dime or a care in the world.
BARNEY SELLERS/Photographer

If you can imagine Rudolph Valentino, Marilyn Monroe, James Dean, Mario Lanza, Judy Garland and Bix Beiderbecke all combined into one corporate super tragic-star, you will get at least some idea of his hold on those to whom he belonged. What has died is, the adolescence of an entire generation.
PETER CLAYTON/Sunday Telegraph

I used my first paycheck to make a down payment on a shirt.
ELVIS

*O*n the day Elvis Presley died, a scorched Las Vegas had for months been praying for rain. Because of the near-drought, water was served in restaurants only "on request", at the moment news came over the radio of the death of Elvis, rain began to fall, there wasn't thunder . . . . there was no lightning, but there was heavy constant rain for hours; drenching the parched earth, it was as though the heavens were crying for a beautiful legend who had made so many others happy, but never found contentment for himself.

EUNICE FIELD/*Showbiz Writer*

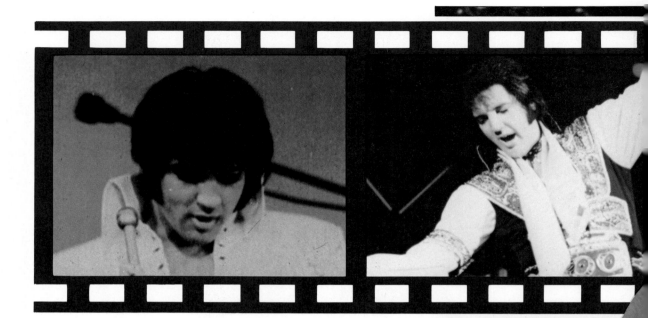

*W*hen we first came to town, these guys like Dean Martin and Frank Sinatra and all these people wanted to come over and hang around with us simply because we had all the women. We didn't want to meet these people, they don't really like us; we don't really like or admire them. The only person we wanted to meet was Elvis Presley. We can't tell you what a thrill it was last night.

JOHN LENNON *(talking to Memphis Mafia)*

I don't like to be called 'Elvis the Pelvis', it's a childish expression.

ELVIS

*E*lvis Presley is morally insane. The spirit of Presleyism has taken down all the bars and standards. Because of this man we are living in a day of jellyfish morality.

Reverend CARL E ELGENA/Pastor, Baptist Church, Des Moines

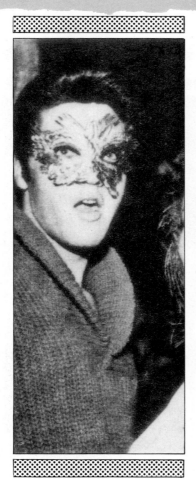

*E*lvis arrived on the scene when the young needed a romantic image. He filled the bill and on top of that, he can sing.
MARLENE DIETRICH

I want to entertain people. That's my whole life to my last breath.
ELVIS/1962

Elvis was in a spending mood, and Vernon was having a relapse as he always did when Elvis got his cheque book out. He asked me what colour car I wanted, I couldn't think for a while I'd never had a new car. A few hours later a brand new car arrived, Elvis apologised because he couldn't get the right colour, I just burst into tears which made Elvis cry.

VESTER PRESLEY/Elvis's Uncle

If Elvis had not dyed his hair black, he would probably had completely white hair just like his daddy, Elvis died clutching a book on christianity about the 'Turin Shroud'.

LARRY GELLER/Elvis's Hairdresser

Elvis was the original punk, I would not have had a musical career without him, in fact every pop singer or group today borrowed from Elvis, and if they say they didn't they're liars.

GARY GLITTER/British Singer/1985

If you want to be attractive to girls then you should never laugh, you just can't look sexy when you smile.

ELVIS/1956

*U*neasy lies the head that
wears the crown.
SHAKESPEARE

Is it a sausage? It is certainly smooth and damp looking, but whoever heard of a 172lb. sausage six foot tall? Is it a Walt Disney goldfish? It has the same sort of big, soft, beautiful eyes and long curly lashes, but whoever heard of a goldfish with sideburns? Is it a corpse? The fact it just hangs there, limp and white with it's little drop-seat mouth, rather like Lord Byron in the wax museum. . . . but suddenly the figure comes to life. The lips part, the eyes half close, the clutched guitar begins to undulate back and forth in an uncomfortably suggestive manner, and wham! The mid section of the body jolts forward to jump and grind and beat out a low down rhythm that take it's pace from boogie and hillbilly rock and roll and something known only to Elvis and his pelvis.
TIME MAGAZINE CRITIC

The most fun I had in Hollywood, was a visit to the Long Beach amusement park when I won eight teddy bears before I had to quit because so many kids followed me.
ELVIS

Most singers and guitar players pat their foot, but Elvis just shakes his leg. He just keeps time that way.
SCOTTY MOORE

Elvis Presley is unspeakably untalented and vulgar just short of true obscenity.
JOHN CROSBY/New York Herald Tribune

Its like someone just came up and told me there aren't going to be any more cheeseburgers in the world.
FELTON JARVIS